ILLINOIS TEST PREP

PARCC Practice Book

Mathematics

Grade 4

ISBN 978-1502436788

CONTENTS

INTRODUCTION
For Parents, Teachers, and Tutors

About the PARCC Assessments

Students in Illinois will be assessed each year by taking a set of tests known as the PARCC assessments. The two main assessments are the Performance-Based Assessment (PBA) and the End-of-Year Assessment (EOY). This book has two complete PBA practice tests and two complete EOY practice tests. The practice tests have the same format, the same question types, and cover the same skills as the real assessments. Further information on the PBA and the EOY is included in the introduction to each practice test.

Key Features of the PARCC Assessments

The PARCC assessments have key features that students will need to be familiar with, including new question styles and formats. These key features are described below.

- The tests are based on the Common Core State Standards and are strongly focused on showing an in-depth understanding of the skills described in the standards.
- The tests include a wider range of question types. There are more constructed response questions, more rigorous selected response questions, more questions involving advanced tasks, and more questions that involve providing explanations or justifying answers.
- The tests are taken online and include computer-based questions. These involve tasks like ordering numbers, selecting points on a number line or graph, sorting items, completing number sentences and equations, and using fraction models.
- The tests include more multi-step problems, more questions that involve applying skills in real-world contexts, and questions that involve complex procedures.

This book has been specifically designed to prepare students for these key features. The questions have a wide range of formats, including questions that mimic the computer-based formats. The questions are more rigorous and include more advanced tasks. The skills assessed match the PARCC tests, with a greater focus on applying skills and on demonstrating in-depth understanding.

About the Common Core State Standards

The state of Illinois has adopted the Common Core State Standards. These standards describe the skills that students are expected to have. Student learning is based on these standards, and all the questions on the PARCC assessments assess these standards. Just like the real PARCC assessments, the questions in this book test whether students have the knowledge and skills described in the Common Core State Standards.

INTRODUCTION TO THE PBA PRACTICE TEST
For Parents, Teachers, and Tutors

About the Performance-Based Assessment

The Performance-Based Assessment (PBA) is taken after about 75% of the school year is complete. The PBA focuses on applying skills and concepts to solve problems. The emphasis is on completing multi-step problems and advanced tasks. This test is made up of three different types of items, as described below.

- **Type I** – these items are straightforward selected response or simple computer-based questions. These items are worth 1 or 2 points.

- **Type II** – these items are constructed response questions that involve completing more complex tasks and usually require students to show their work, explain their answer, or provide justifications. These items are worth 3 or 4 points.

- **Type III** – these items are complex constructed response questions that involve modeling or applying skills in real-world contexts. These items are worth 3 or 6 points.

The actual test contains 10 Type I items, 4 Type II items, and 3 Type III items. The practice tests in this book contains more questions of each type, especially more Type II and Type III items. This will ensure that students experience all the types of questions they are likely to encounter on the real test and gain the experience needed to complete more rigorous tasks.

Taking the Test

Just like the real EOY test, the practice test is divided into two sessions. Each session includes 15 questions. On the real test, students are allowed 2 hours to complete each session. To account for the additional questions, students should be allowed 4 hours for each session of the practice test. Students can complete the two sessions on the same day or on different days, but should have a break between sessions.

Calculators and Tools

Students should be provided with a ruler and a protractor to use on both sessions of the test. Students are not allowed to use a calculator on any session of the PARCC tests, and so should complete all the practice tests without the use of a calculator.

PARCC Performance-Based Assessment

Practice Test 1

Session 1

Instructions

Read each question carefully. For each multiple-choice question, fill in the circle for the correct answer. For other types of questions, follow the directions given in the question.

Some questions may ask you to show your work. Be sure to show your work or explain how you found your answer in the space provided.

You may use a ruler and a protractor to help you answer questions. You may not use a calculator on this test.

1   Look at the letters below. Circle **all** the letters that have a line of symmetry.

A C F J P R T W Z

2   What kind of angle is each internal angle of the shape below?

   Ⓐ   Acute

   Ⓑ   Right

   Ⓒ   Obtuse

   Ⓓ   Straight

3   Donna bought a lollipop for $0.60 and a candy for $0.15. How much change would Donna receive from $1?

   Ⓐ $0.15

   Ⓑ $0.25

   Ⓒ $0.35

   Ⓓ $0.75

4   Sandra started walking to school at 8:45 a.m. It took her 25 minutes to get to school. What time did she get to school?

Ⓐ   9:00 a.m.

Ⓑ   9:10 a.m.

Ⓒ   9:15 a.m.

Ⓓ   9:20 a.m.

5   The table below shows the shirt number of six players on a basketball team.

Player	Shirt Number
Don	12
Jamie	17
Curtis	22
Chan	9
Wendell	31
Kevin	49

Determine whether each player's shirt number is prime or composite. Write P or C on the lines below to show your choice.

____ Don   ____ Jamie   ____ Curtis

____ Chan   ____ Wendell   ____ Kevin

6   Which shaded model represents $\frac{5}{4}$?

7   The numbers below are arranged from least to greatest.

$$1{,}098 \quad 2{,}269 \quad \underline{\hspace{3em}} \quad 2{,}350 \quad 2{,}699$$

Which **two** numbers could go on the blank line?

☐   2,800

☐   2,401

☐   2,320

☐   2,185

☐   2,280

☐   2,239

8   Jenna buys 8 packets of letter paper. Each packet contains 12 sheets of paper. She uses 16 sheets of letter paper a week. How many weeks will it take her to use all the letter paper?

Show your work.

Answer _____ weeks

9 Kenneth got on a train at 9:30 in the morning. He got off the train at 1:20 in the afternoon. How long was Kenneth on the train for?

Show your work.

Answer _____ hours _____ minutes

10   A fish tank can hold 20 liters of water. How many milliliters of water can the fish tank hold?

Show your work.

Answer _____ ml

11 The table below shows the number of meals a café served on four different days.

Monday	Tuesday	Wednesday	Thursday
1,487	1,510	1,461	1,469

Part A

Place the numbers in order from the least to the most number of meals served.

_____ < _____ < _____ < _____

Part B

On Friday, the café served 200 more meals than on Tuesday. How many meals did the café serve on Friday?

Show your work.

Answer _____

12 The table below shows the number of male and female students at Hill Street School.

Gender	Number
Male	2,629
Female	2,518

Part A
How many students go to the school in all?

Show your work.

Answer _____

Part B
How many more male students are there than female students?

Show your work.

Answer _____

13 A right triangle is shown below.

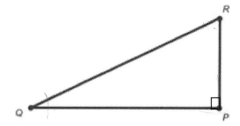

If angle *Q* measures 35°, what is the measure of angle *R*?

Show your work.

Answer _____°

14 The top of Kevin's dining room table is 4 feet long and 3 feet wide. Kevin wants to cover the middle of the table with tiles. He plans to leave a 6 inch border around the edge of the table and tile the center. How many square feet of tiles will he need? Use the diagram below to help you find the answer.

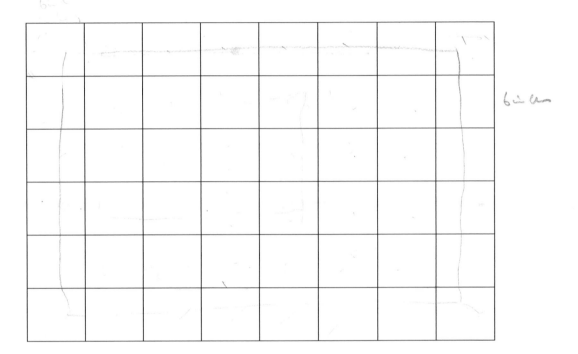

Answer _____ square feet

15   What are all the common factors of 10, 20, and 40?

Show your work.

Answer _____

On the lines below, explain why all the factors of 10 are also factors of 20 and 40.

_____

_____

_____

_____

_____

END OF SESSION 1

PARCC Performance-Based Assessment

Practice Test 1

Session 2

Instructions

Read each question carefully. For each multiple-choice question, fill in the circle for the correct answer. For other types of questions, follow the directions given in the question.

Some questions may ask you to show your work. Be sure to show your work or explain how you found your answer in the space provided.

You may use a ruler and a protractor to help you answer questions. You may not use a calculator on this test.

16 Megan arranged some beads in the pattern shown below. Draw the correct two beads that continue the pattern below.

17 Which shaded model shows a fraction greater than $\frac{4}{5}$?

Ⓐ

Ⓑ

Ⓒ

Ⓓ

18 What is the number 457,869 rounded to the nearest ten thousand and the nearest thousand? Write your answers below.

Nearest ten thousand: _____

Nearest thousand: _____

19 Which is the best estimate of the length of a football?

Ⓐ 10 inches

Ⓑ 10 millimeters

Ⓒ 10 meters

Ⓓ 10 yards

20 Mia bought a milkshake. She was given the change shown below. How much change was Mia given? Write your answer below.

$ _____

21 Which number has a 4 in the millions place?

Ⓐ   8,340,386

Ⓑ   5,468,950

Ⓒ   4,082,663

Ⓓ   8,934,159

22 Which figure below shows a line of symmetry?

Ⓐ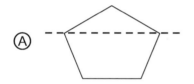

Ⓑ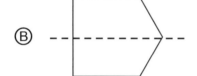

Ⓒ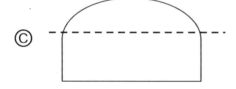

Ⓓ

23 Look at the number line below.

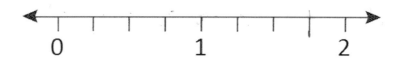

Part A

Plot the decimal 1.75 on the number line.

Part B

What fraction is equivalent to 1.75?

Answer _____

Explain how you found your answer.

_____

_____

_____

_____

_____

24   Look at the model below.

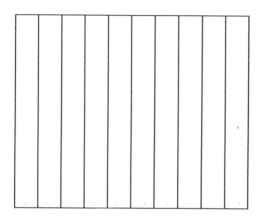 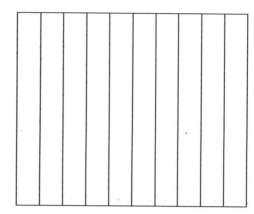

Part A

Shade the model to show $1\frac{7}{10}$.

Part B

Write the mixed number $1\frac{7}{10}$ as an improper fraction.

Answer _____

On the lines below, explain how you found your answer.

_____

_____

_____

_____

_____

25 Look at the number pattern below.

$$5, 11, 17, 23, 29, 35, \_\_\_\_$$

Part A

If the pattern continues, which number will come next?

Answer _____

Part B

Explain how you found your answer.

_____

_____

_____

Part C

Will all the numbers in the pattern be odd numbers? Explain your answer.

_____

_____

_____

26   Salma drew these shapes.

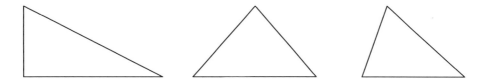

Part A

Identify the shape that has a line of symmetry. Draw the line of symmetry on the shape you identified.

Part B

On the lines below, describe how you can tell that the shape has a line of symmetry.

_____

_____

_____

_____

_____

27 **Part A**

Identify the place value for each digit in the number 234.15.
Draw a line to match each digit with its place value.

1   hundreds

2   hundredths

3   ones

4   tens

5   tenths

Part B

In the space below, write the number 234.15 in expanded form.

28 A school divided its grade 4 students into 6 classes. There were exactly 26 students in each class. How many students were there in all?

Show your work.

Answer _____

29   A park has a length of 60 feet and a width of 40 feet. What is the area of the park?

Show your work.

Answer _____ square feet

30 Sort the figures below by placing the correct letters in each column of the table.

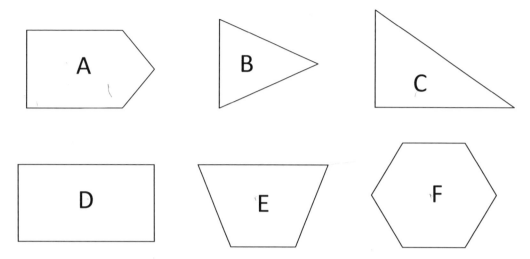

1 or more right angles	1 or more pairs of parallel sides	1 or more pairs of perpendicular sides

END OF SESSION 2

INTRODUCTION TO THE EOY PRACTICE TEST
For Parents, Teachers, and Tutors

About the End-of-Year Assessment

The End-of-Year Assessment (EOY) is taken after about 90% of the school year is complete. It is designed to allow students to demonstrate that they have the skills and knowledge described in the Common Core State Standards. The EOY Assessment only includes the Type I questions described below.

- **Type I** – these items are straightforward selected response or simple computer-based questions. These items are worth 1 or 2 points.

These items may be simple selected response questions where the one correct answer is selected or selected response questions with 2 or more correct answers. The computer-based questions could involve writing numerical answers, sorting or ordering numbers or items, selecting points on a number line or graph, completing number sentences and equations, or using fraction models. This practice test includes a wide range of formats that mimic the computer-based questions.

The actual test contains 36 Type I items. The practice tests in this book contain 50 Type I items. This will ensure that students have practice with all the types of questions they are likely to encounter on the real test and gain the experience needed to complete questions with a range of new formats.

Taking the Test

Just like the real EOY test, the practice test is divided into two sessions. Each session includes 25 questions. On the real test, students are allowed 2 hours to complete each session. To account for the additional questions, students should be allowed 3 hours for each session of the practice test. Students can complete the two sessions on the same day or on different days, but should have a break between sessions.

Calculators and Tools

Students should be provided with a ruler and a protractor to use on both sessions of the test. Students are not allowed to use a calculator on any session of the PARCC tests, and so should complete all the practice tests without the use of a calculator.

PARCC End-of-Year Assessment

Practice Test 1

Session 1

Instructions

Read each question carefully. For each multiple-choice question, fill in the circle for the correct answer. For other types of questions, follow the directions given in the question.

You may use a ruler and a protractor to help you answer questions. You may not use a calculator on this test.

1   What is the perimeter and area of the rectangle? Write your answers below.

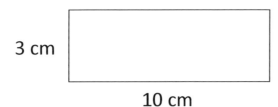

3 cm

10 cm

Perimeter: _____

Area: _____

2   An array for the number 36 is shown below.

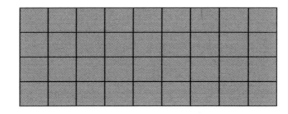

Which numbers are factors of 36? Select **all** the correct answers.

☐   4

☐   5

☐   7

☐   8

☐   9

3   The table below shows the cost of food at a diner.

Drinks		Meals	
Small milkshake	$1.80	Plain hamburger	$3.50
Large milkshake	$2.00	Chicken burger	$4.20
Small soda	$1.10	Hotdog	$2.60
Large soda	$1.50	Meatball sub	$3.10
Fruit juice	$1.90	Quiche	$2.10

Lisa bought two different items and spent exactly $4.00. Circle the **two** items that Lisa bought.

Small milkshake   Plain hamburger

Large milkshake   Chicken burger

Small soda   Hotdog

Large soda   Meatball sub

Fruit juice   Quiche

4   The table below shows the entry cost for a museum.

Adult	$10 per person
Child	$8 per person
Family (2 adults and 2 children)	$30 per family

How much would a family of 2 adults and 2 children save by buying a family ticket instead of individual tickets?

Ⓐ $2

Ⓑ $6

Ⓒ $8

Ⓓ $10

5   Maria is reading a book with 286 pages. She has read 38 pages. To the nearest ten, how many pages does Maria have left to read?

Ⓐ   240

Ⓑ   250

Ⓒ   260

Ⓓ   270

6   A box of beads contains 240 beads. Chang buys 4 boxes of beads. How many beads did Chang buy? Write your answer below.

_____ beads

7   Liam has 6 pots he grows herbs in. He planted mint in $\frac{1}{4}$ of each pot. What fraction of a pot is the mint in total?

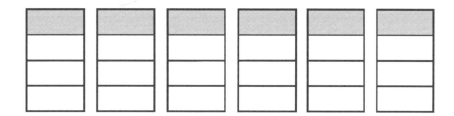

Ⓐ $1\frac{1}{2}$ pots

Ⓑ $1\frac{1}{4}$ pots

Ⓒ $1\frac{1}{6}$ pots

Ⓓ $1\frac{1}{8}$ pots

8 What is the measure of the angle shown below? Write your answer below.

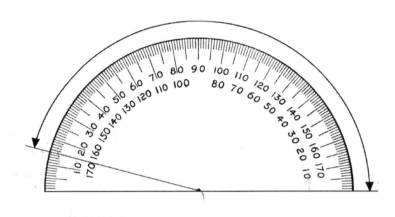

_____°

9 A pet shop sells fish for $3 each. The pet shop sold $96 worth of fish one day. How many fish did the pet shop sell that day?

Ⓐ   32

Ⓑ   36

Ⓒ   48

Ⓓ   288

10 Which number is a factor of 57?

Ⓐ   11

Ⓑ   13

Ⓒ   17

Ⓓ   19

11 Which numbers are multiples of 6? Circle **all** the correct numbers.

2	3	12	20
24	30	44	46
50	54	66	70

12 A motorbike has a weight of 255 kilograms. What is the weight of the motorbike in grams? Write your answer below.

_____ grams

13 The fraction $\frac{56}{100}$ is plotted on the number line below. What decimal is plotted on the number line?

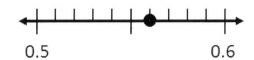

0.5   0.6

Ⓐ   5.6

Ⓑ   5.06

Ⓒ   0.56

Ⓓ   0.506

14 The table shows the relationship between feet and inches. Complete the table by showing how many feet would have a value of 72 inches.

Feet	Inches
1	12
2	24
3	36
	72

15   The angle that is formed between two lines has a measure of 95°.
Which term describes this angle?

    Ⓐ   Acute

    Ⓑ   Right

    Ⓒ   Obtuse

    Ⓓ   Straight

16   Jayden wants to find the length of a paperclip. Which unit would
Jayden be best to use?

    Ⓐ   Yards

    Ⓑ   Feet

    Ⓒ   Kilometers

    Ⓓ   Centimeters

17 There are 1,920 students at Jenna's school. Which of these is another way to write 1,920?

Ⓐ   1,000 + 900 + 20

Ⓑ   1,000 + 900 + 2

Ⓒ   1,000 + 90 + 20

Ⓓ   1,000 + 90 + 2

18 Which of the following describes the rule for this pattern?

1, 3, 6, 8, 11, 13, 16

Ⓐ   Add 2, add 3

Ⓑ   Add 2, multiply by 2

Ⓒ   Multiply by 3, multiply by 2

Ⓓ   Multiply by 3, add 3

19 Troy swapped 2 quarters for coins with the same value. Which of these could Troy have swapped his 2 quarters for? Select **all** the correct answers.

☐¹ 25 pennies

☐² 20 nickels

☐³ 10 nickels

☐⁴ 10 dimes

☐⁵ 4 nickels and 4 dimes

☐⁶ 4 dimes and 10 pennies

20 Which number goes in the box to make the equation below true? Write your answer in the box below.

$$54 \div \boxed{} = 9$$

21 A pumpkin weighs 4 pounds. How many ounces does the pumpkin weigh?

  Ⓐ   32 ounces

  Ⓑ   40 ounces

  Ⓒ   48 ounces

  Ⓓ   64 ounces

22 The table below shows the population of 3 towns.

Town	Population
Franklin	18,725
Torine	24,214
Maxville	16,722

Which number sentence shows the best way to estimate how much greater the population of Torine is than Franklin?

  Ⓐ   24,000 − 16,000 = 8,000

  Ⓑ   24,000 − 17,000 = 7,000

  Ⓒ   24,000 − 18,000 = 6,000

  Ⓓ   24,000 − 19,000 = 5,000

23 A movie made $5,256,374 in its first weekend. What does the 2 in this number represent?

    Ⓐ   Two thousand

    Ⓑ   Twenty thousand

    Ⓒ   Two hundred thousand

    Ⓓ   Two million

24 Select **all** the shapes that have at least one line of symmetry.

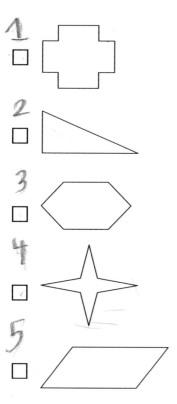

25   The table shows the amount Davis spent on phone calls each month.

Month	Amount
April	$9.22
May	$9.09
June	$9.18
July	$9.05

In which month did Davis spend the least on phone calls?

Ⓐ   April

Ⓑ   May

Ⓒ   June

Ⓓ   July

END OF SESSION 1

PARCC End-of-Year Assessment

Practice Test 1

Session 2

Instructions

Read each question carefully. For each multiple-choice question, fill in the circle for the correct answer. For other types of questions, follow the directions given in the question.

You may use a ruler and a protractor to help you answer questions. You may not use a calculator on this test.

26 Emma grouped a set of numbers into two groups, as shown below.

Group 1	Group 2
14	21
86	79
922	325
388	683

Circle all the numbers that should be placed in Group 2.

18   630   864   57

247   121   156   93

27 The sizes of the drill bits in a set are measured in inches. Which size drill bits are greater than $\frac{1}{2}$ inch? Select **all** the correct answers.

☐ $\frac{3}{8}$ inch

☐ $\frac{7}{16}$ inch

☐ $\frac{1}{8}$ inch

☐ $\frac{9}{16}$ inch

☐ $\frac{7}{12}$ inch

28 What is the rule to find the value of a term in the sequence below?

Position, n	Value of Term
1	3
2	4
3	5
4	6
5	7

Ⓐ $2n$

Ⓑ $3n$

Ⓒ $n + 2$

Ⓓ $n + 3$

29 A square garden has side lengths of 8 inches. What is the area of the garden? Write your answer below. Be sure to include the correct units.

_____

30   Look at the line segments shown below.

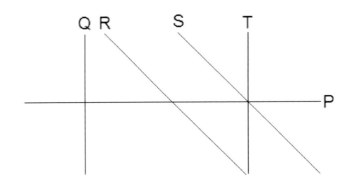

Which **two** pairs of line segments are parallel? Write your answers below.

Line segments _____ and _____

Line segments _____ and _____

31   Which of these is the best estimate of the length of a baseball bat?

Ⓐ   3 inches

Ⓑ   3 feet

Ⓒ   3 millimeters

Ⓓ   3 centimeters

32 There are 40,260 people watching a baseball game. Which of these is another way to write 40,260?

Ⓐ   4 + 2 + 6

Ⓑ   40 + 2 + 60

Ⓒ   40,000 + 200 + 6

Ⓓ   40,000 + 200 + 60

33 The model below is shaded to show $2\frac{4}{10}$.

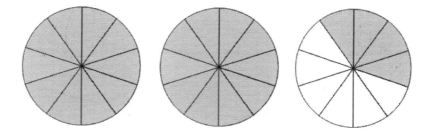

What decimal does the model represent? Write your answer below.

_____

34 Which of the following is another way to write the numeral 600,032?

Ⓐ Six hundred thousand and thirty-two

Ⓑ Six million and thirty-two

Ⓒ Six hundred and thirty-two

Ⓓ Six thousand and thirty-two

35 The drawing below shows a kite.

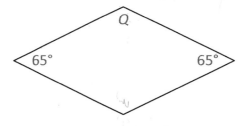

Not drawn to scale

What is the measure of angle Q?

Ⓐ 57.5°

Ⓑ 65°

Ⓒ 115°

Ⓓ 230°

36   Which numbers are composite numbers? Select **all** the correct answers.

☐   67

☐   73

☐   77

☐   81

☐   89

☐   91

37   What is 83,462 rounded to the nearest hundred and the nearest ten? Write your answers below.

Nearest hundred: _____

Nearest ten: _____

38   Which **two** pairs of numbers complete the equation below?

$$\boxed{} \times 100 = \boxed{}$$

☐   60 and 600

☐   60 and 6,000

☐   60 and 60,000

☐   6 and 60

☐   6 and 600

☐   6 and 6000

39   What is the measure of the angle shown below?

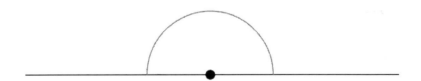

Ⓐ   45°

Ⓑ   90°

Ⓒ   100°

Ⓓ   180°

40 Kai found the coins shown below in the sofa. What is the value of the coins that Kai found? Write your answer below.

$ _____

41 Which figure below does NOT have any parallel sides?

Ⓐ

Ⓑ

Ⓒ

Ⓓ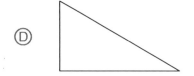

42   What is another way to write the fraction $\frac{9}{4}$?

Ⓐ $1\frac{1}{4}$

Ⓑ $1\frac{3}{4}$

Ⓒ $2\frac{1}{4}$

Ⓓ $2\frac{3}{4}$

43   Jackie made this table to show how much she received in tips on the four days that she worked. On which day did Jackie earn closest to $32?

Day	Amount
Monday	$32.55
Tuesday	$31.98
Thursday	$30.75
Friday	$32.09

Ⓐ   Monday

Ⓑ   Tuesday

Ⓒ   Thursday

Ⓓ   Friday

44 Bruce is counting his quarters. He puts them in 35 piles of 5. How could you work out the total value of the quarters?

  Ⓐ Divide 35 by 5, and multiply the result by $0.25

  Ⓑ Multiply 35 by 5, and multiply the result by $0.25

  Ⓒ Divide 35 by 5, and divide the result by $0.25

  Ⓓ Multiply 35 by 5, and divide the result by $0.25

45 A bakery makes muffins in batches of 12. The bakery made 18 batches of muffins. Which is the best estimate of the number of muffins made?

  Ⓐ 100

  Ⓑ 400

  Ⓒ 250

  Ⓓ 200

46 Katie saw the sign below at a fruit stand.

If Katie spent $6 on oranges, how many oranges would she get? Write your answer on the line below.

_____

47 The normal price of a CD player is $298. During a sale, the CD player was $45 less than the normal price. What was the sale price of the CD player?

   Ⓐ $343

   Ⓑ $333

   Ⓒ $263

   Ⓓ $253

48 What is the product of 8 and 9? Write your answer below.

_____

49   Bagels are sold in packets of 4 or packets of 6. Kieran needs to buy exactly 32 bagels. Which set of packets could Kieran buy?

Ⓐ   2 packets of 4 bagels and 4 packets of 6 bagels

Ⓑ   3 packets of 4 bagels and 3 packets of 6 bagels

Ⓒ   4 packets of 4 bagels and 2 packets of 6 bagels

Ⓓ   5 packets of 4 bagels and 1 packet of 6 bagels

50   A bakery needs to order 60 eggs. There are 12 eggs in each carton. Which number sentence could be used to find c, the number of cartons the bakery should order?

Ⓐ $12 \times c = 60$

Ⓑ $12 \div c = 60$

Ⓒ $60 - 12 = c$

Ⓓ $60 \times 12 = c$

END OF SESSION 2

INTRODUCTION TO THE PBA PRACTICE TEST
For Parents, Teachers, and Tutors

About the Performance-Based Assessment

The Performance-Based Assessment (PBA) is taken after about 75% of the school year is complete. The PBA focuses on applying skills and concepts to solve problems. The emphasis is on completing multi-step problems and advanced tasks. This test is made up of three different types of items, as described below.

- **Type I** – these items are straightforward selected response or simple computer-based questions. These items are worth 1 or 2 points.

- **Type II** – these items are constructed response questions that involve completing more complex tasks and usually require students to show their work, explain their answer, or provide justifications. These items are worth 3 or 4 points.

- **Type III** – these items are complex constructed response questions that involve modeling or applying skills in real-world contexts. These items are worth 3 or 6 points.

The actual test contains 10 Type I items, 4 Type II items, and 3 Type III items. The practice tests in this book contains more questions of each type, especially more Type II and Type III items. This will ensure that students experience all the types of questions they are likely to encounter on the real test and gain the experience needed to complete more rigorous tasks.

Taking the Test

Just like the real EOY test, the practice test is divided into two sessions. Each session includes 15 questions. On the real test, students are allowed 2 hours to complete each session. To account for the additional questions, students should be allowed 4 hours for each session of the practice test. Students can complete the two sessions on the same day or on different days, but should have a break between sessions.

Calculators and Tools

Students should be provided with a ruler and a protractor to use on both sessions of the test. Students are not allowed to use a calculator on any session of the PARCC tests, and so should complete all the practice tests without the use of a calculator.

PARCC Performance-Based Assessment

Practice Test 2

Session 1

Instructions

Read each question carefully. For each multiple-choice question, fill in the circle for the correct answer. For other types of questions, follow the directions given in the question.

Some questions may ask you to show your work. Be sure to show your work or explain how you found your answer in the space provided.

You may use a ruler and a protractor to help you answer questions. You may not use a calculator on this test.

1   Which measurement is the best estimate of the length of a swimming pool?

   Ⓐ   10 millimeters

   Ⓑ   10 centimeters

   Ⓒ   10 kilometers

   Ⓓ   10 meters

2   Circle **all** the angles of the shapes below that are obtuse.

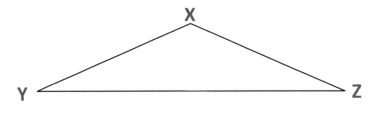

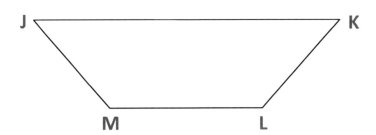

3   What part of the model is shaded?

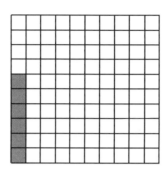

   Ⓐ   6.0

   Ⓑ   0.6

   Ⓒ   0.06

   Ⓓ   0.006

4   Which value of *p* makes the equation below true?

$$p \div 7 = 9$$

   Ⓐ   49

   Ⓑ   56

   Ⓒ   63

   Ⓓ   81

5   Shade the **two** diagrams below to represent fractions equivalent to $\frac{1}{2}$.

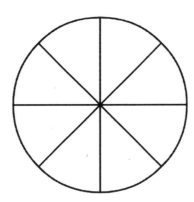

6   What is the rule to find the value of a term in the sequence below?

Position, *n*	Value of Term
1	3
2	6
3	9
4	12

Ⓐ $n \times 2$

Ⓑ $n \times 3$

Ⓒ $n + 2$

Ⓓ $n + 3$

7   Which statements are true? Select **all** the correct statements.

☐   386 > 389

☐   412 > 450

☐   589 < 596

☐   611 < 610

☐   805 > 799

☐   465 > 481

☐   987 < 937

☐   152 < 170

8　What is the sum of $\frac{1}{10}$ and $\frac{3}{100}$?

Show your work.

Answer _____

9   Mrs. Smyth has 82 colored pencils. She wants to divide them evenly between 8 people. How many whole pencils will each person receive?

Show your work.

Answer _____ pencils

10 The table below shows the number of students in each grade at the David Hall School.

Grade	Number of Students
3	254
4	235
5	229

How many students are there in all?

Show your work.

Answer _____

11 The diagram below represents the sum of $\frac{1}{4}$, $\frac{1}{4}$, and $\frac{1}{4}$.

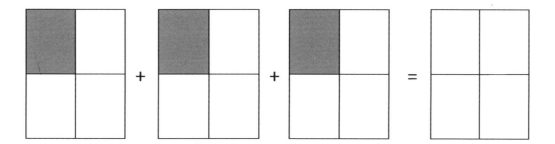

Part A

Shade the last grid to show the sum of $\frac{1}{4}$, $\frac{1}{4}$, and $\frac{1}{4}$.

Part B

What is the sum of $\frac{1}{4}$, $\frac{1}{4}$, and $\frac{1}{4}$?

Answer _____

On the lines below, explain how the diagram helped you find the sum.

_____

_____

_____

_____

_____

12   What is the area of the square shown below?

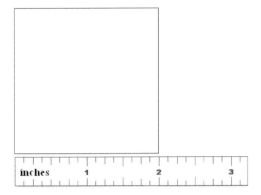

Show your work.

Answer _____

13   Jeremy had the coins shown below.

He swapped all the coins for nickels of the same total value. How many nickels should he have received?

Show your work.

Answer _____ nickels

14   A trapezoid is shown below.

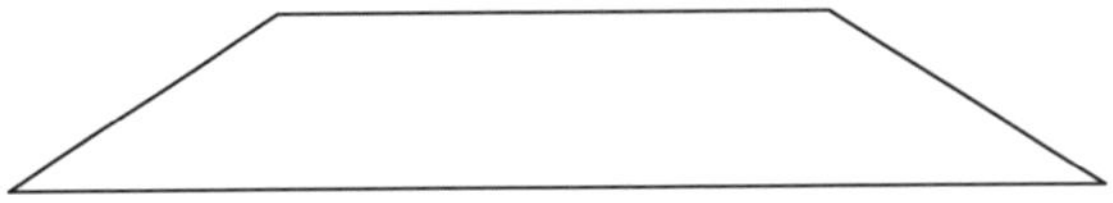

Part A
Circle **all** the acute angles of the trapezoid above.

Part B
On the lines below, explain how you can determine whether the angles are acute without measuring them.

_____

_____

_____

_____

15   The fine for having a DVD overdue is a basic fee of $4 plus an additional $2 for each day that the movie is overdue.

Part A

Complete the equation below to show c, the amount of the fine in dollars when a DVD is overdue for d days.

$$c = \underline{\hspace{1cm}} d + \underline{\hspace{1cm}}$$

Part B

Use the equation from Part A to find the cost of the fine when a DVD is overdue for 6 days.

Show your work.

Answer $\$\underline{\hspace{2cm}}$

END OF SESSION 2

PARCC Performance-Based Assessment

Practice Test 2

Session 2

Instructions

Read each question carefully. For each multiple-choice question, fill in the circle for the correct answer. For other types of questions, follow the directions given in the question.

Some questions may ask you to show your work. Be sure to show your work or explain how you found your answer in the space provided.

You may use a ruler and a protractor to help you answer questions. You may not use a calculator on this test.

---

16 The table below shows the total number of pieces of bread Aaron used to make peanut butter and jelly sandwiches.

Number of Sandwiches	Number of Pieces of Bread
2	6
4	12
8	24

Complete the missing number to show the relationship between the number of sandwiches and the number of pieces of bread.

Sandwiches × ☐ = pieces of bread

17 Which unit would be best to use to measure the length of a box of tissues?

Ⓐ   Yards

Ⓑ   Miles

Ⓒ   Centimeters

Ⓓ   Kilometers

18   Which **two** numbers are multiples of 8? Select the **two** correct answers.

☐   2

☐   4

☐   18

☐   32

☐   36

☐   56

19   What is the sum of $1\frac{3}{4}$ and $\frac{1}{2}$? Complete the diagram below to help you find the answer.

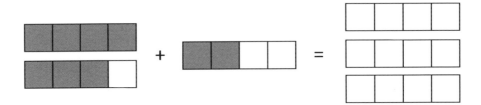

Ⓐ   2

Ⓑ $2\frac{1}{4}$

Ⓒ $2\frac{1}{2}$

Ⓓ $2\frac{3}{4}$

20 Joseph earns $8 per hour. In one week, he earned $280. How many hours did Joseph work that week? Write your answer below.

_____ hours

21 Which is the best estimate of the angle between the hands of the clock?

Ⓐ   15°

Ⓑ   45°

Ⓒ   75°

Ⓓ   90°

22 It took Bianca 3 hours and 10 minutes to travel to her aunt's house. How long did the trip take in minutes?

Ⓐ   160 minutes

Ⓑ   180 minutes

Ⓒ   190 minutes

Ⓓ   310 minutes

23 Jed has 12 dimes, 18 nickels, and 24 pennies. He wants to divide them into as many piles as possible, but he wants the same number of dimes, nickels, and pennies in each pile.

Part A
What is the greatest number of equal piles Jed can divide the coins into?

Show your work.

Answer _____

Part B
If Jed divides the coins into those equal piles, how many pennies will be in each pile?

Show your work.

Answer _____

24 In the space below, sketch and label a right angle, an acute angle, and an obtuse angle.

Right Angle

Acute Angle

Obtuse Angle

Which angle sketched had to be an exact angle measure? Explain your answer.

_____

_____

_____

_____

25   Emma grouped the numbers from 10 to 20 into prime and composite numbers.

Prime	Composite
11	10
13	12
17	14
19	15
	16
	18
	20

Which numbers from 21 to 30 should Emma add to the list of prime numbers? List the numbers below.

Answer _____

Explain how the prime numbers are different from composite numbers.

_____

_____

_____

_____

26 A rectangular park has a length of 80 feet and a width of 40 feet.

Part A

What is the perimeter of the park in feet?

Show your work.

Answer _____ feet

Part B

What is the perimeter of the park in yards?

Show your work.

Answer _____ yards

27 Use the model below to find the sum of $\frac{3}{10}$ and $\frac{17}{100}$.

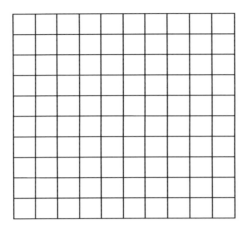

Answer _____

28 Ben answered $\frac{70}{100}$ of the questions on a test correctly. What decimal is equivalent to $\frac{70}{100}$?

Show your work.

Answer _____

29 Trevor's baby sister had a nap for $1\frac{3}{4}$ hours. How many minutes did she nap for?

Show your work.

Answer _____ minutes

30　**Part A**

Circle **all** the statements that correctly describe the rhombus below.

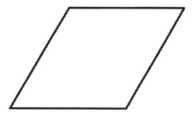

2 pairs of parallel sides

2 pairs of perpendicular sides

4 equal angles

4 right angles

4 congruent sides

Part B

Write the name of the shape that is described by **all** the statements above.

Answer _____

END OF SESSION 2

INTRODUCTION TO THE EOY PRACTICE TEST
For Parents, Teachers, and Tutors

About the End-of-Year Assessment

The End-of-Year Assessment (EOY) is taken after about 90% of the school year is complete. It is designed to allow students to demonstrate that they have the skills and knowledge described in the Common Core State Standards. The EOY Assessment only includes the Type I questions described below.

- **Type I** – these items are straightforward selected response or simple computer-based questions. These items are worth 1 or 2 points.

These items may be simple selected response questions where the one correct answer is selected or selected response questions with 2 or more correct answers. The computer-based questions could involve writing numerical answers, sorting or ordering numbers or items, selecting points on a number line or graph, completing number sentences and equations, or using fraction models. This practice test includes a wide range of formats that mimic the computer-based questions.

The actual test contains 36 Type I items. The practice tests in this book contain 50 Type I items. This will ensure that students have practice with all the types of questions they are likely to encounter on the real test and gain the experience needed to complete questions with a range of new formats.

Taking the Test

Just like the real EOY test, the practice test is divided into two sessions. Each session includes 25 questions. On the real test, students are allowed 2 hours to complete each session. To account for the additional questions, students should be allowed 3 hours for each session of the practice test. Students can complete the two sessions on the same day or on different days, but should have a break between sessions.

Calculators and Tools

Students should be provided with a ruler and a protractor to use on both sessions of the test. Students are not allowed to use a calculator on any session of the PARCC tests, and so should complete all the practice tests without the use of a calculator.

PARCC End-of-Year Assessment

Practice Test 2

Session 1

Instructions

Read each question carefully. For each multiple-choice question, fill in the circle for the correct answer. For other types of questions, follow the directions given in the question.

You may use a ruler and a protractor to help you answer questions. You may not use a calculator on this test.

---

1   Josephine boarded a train at 10:10 a.m. She got off the train at 12:55 p.m. How many minutes was she on the train for? Write your answer below.

_____ minutes

2   Ari is putting photos in an album. He can fit 6 photos on each page. He has 44 photos to place in the album. If he puts 6 photos on each page and the remainder on the last page, how many photos will be on the last page?

Ⓐ   1

Ⓑ   2

Ⓒ   3

Ⓓ   4

3   Which is a prime factor of the composite number 24?

Ⓐ   8

Ⓑ   7

Ⓒ   6

Ⓓ   3

4 Mia is setting up tables for a party. Each table can seat 6 people. Mia needs to seat 42 people. Mia wants to find how many tables she will need. Complete the equation below that shows how to find the number of tables she will need, *t*.

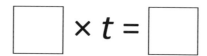

5 Vienna bought a packet of 12 gift cards. She used 2 gift cards and her sister used 3 gift cards. What fraction of the gift cards did the two sisters use?

Ⓐ $\frac{1}{2}$

Ⓑ $\frac{2}{3}$

Ⓒ $\frac{5}{12}$

Ⓓ $\frac{1}{6}$

6 Zoe has 90 small lollipops, 30 large lollipops, and 55 candies. What is a common factor Zoe could use to divide the treats into equal groups? Circle the correct answer.

2   3   5   9   10   15

7   A school cafeteria offered four Italian meal choices. The table below shows the number of meals served of each type.

Meal	Number Served
Pasta	151
Pizza	167
Salad	213
Risotto	117

Which is the best estimate of the total number of meals served?

Ⓐ   630

Ⓑ   650

Ⓒ   660

Ⓓ   670

8   Jay made 8 trays of 6 muffins each. He gave 12 muffins away. Which expression can be used to find how many muffins he had left?

Ⓐ $(8 \times 6) - 12$

Ⓑ $(8 \times 6) + 12$

Ⓒ $8 + 6 - 12$

Ⓓ $8 + 6 + 12$

9   Stevie had $1.45. She bought a drink for $1.20. Stevie was given one coin as change. Which coin should Stevie have been given?

Ⓐ   A dime

Ⓑ   A penny

Ⓒ   A quarter

Ⓓ   A nickel

10   Which of these is the best estimate of the mass of a watermelon?

Ⓐ   5 ounces

Ⓑ   5 grams

Ⓒ   5 pounds

Ⓓ   5 milligrams

11 The factor tree for the number 60 is shown below.

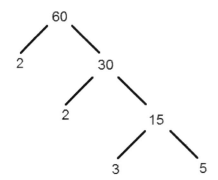

According to the factor tree, which statements are true? Select **all** the correct statements.

☐ The number 30 is a prime number.

☐ The number 60 is a composite number.

☐ The only prime factor of 60 is 2.

☐ The numbers 15 and 30 are prime factors of 60.

☑ The numbers 2, 3, and 5 are prime factors of 60.

☐ The numbers 4 and 6 are factors of 60.

12 Each number that was put into the number machine below changed according to a rule.

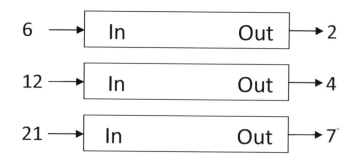

Complete the equation that describes the rule for the number machine. Add the correct symbol to the first box and the correct number to the second box.

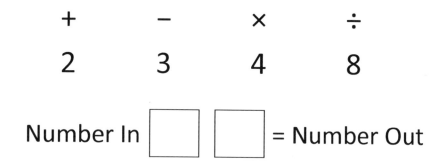

13 Which digit is in the thousands place in the number 6,124,853?

Ⓐ 6

Ⓑ 1

Ⓒ 2

Ⓓ 4

14 Malcolm surveyed some people to find out how many pets they owned. The line plot shows the results of the survey.

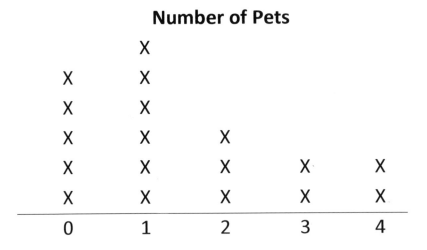

Number of Pets

How many people owned 2 or more pets? Write your answer below.

_____ people

15 The shaded model below represents a fraction.

Shade the model below to represent an equivalent fraction.

16   What decimal does the shaded model below represent? Write your answer below.

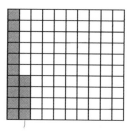

_____

17   The diagram shows two sets of black and white stickers.

Which of these compares the portion of black stickers in each set?

Ⓐ $\frac{8}{9} > \frac{2}{3}$

Ⓑ $\frac{8}{9} < \frac{2}{9}$

Ⓒ $\frac{2}{3} < \frac{1}{3}$

Ⓓ $\frac{1}{9} > \frac{6}{9}$

18 The grade 4 students at Diane's school are collecting cans for a food drive. The table below shows how many cans each class collected.

Class	Number of Cans
Miss Adams	36
Mr. Walsh	28
Mrs. Naroda	47

Which is the best way to estimate the number of cans collected in all?

Ⓐ 30 + 20 + 40 = ?

Ⓑ 30 + 30 + 40 = ?

Ⓒ 40 + 30 + 50 = ?

Ⓓ 40 + 30 + 40 = ?

19 Convert 12 quarts to pints and cups. Write your answers below.

12 quarts = _____ pints

12 quarts = _____ cups

20 Which of these could be two of the angle measures of the right triangle below?

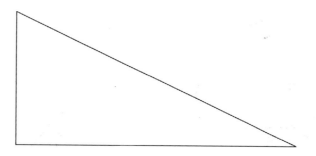

Ⓐ   20° and 60°

Ⓑ   25° and 65°

Ⓒ   30° and 70°

Ⓓ   45° and 75°

21 If *n* is a number in the pattern, which rule can be used to find the next number in the pattern?

4, 6, 8, 10, 12, 14, 16, ...

Ⓐ   *n* + 2

Ⓑ   *n* − 2

Ⓒ   *n* + 4

Ⓓ   *n* − 4

22   What part of the model is shaded?

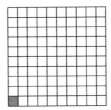

Ⓐ   0.01

Ⓑ   0.1

Ⓒ   1

Ⓓ   10

23   Which of these shapes has exactly one pair of perpendicular sides?

Ⓐ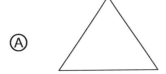

Ⓑ

Ⓒ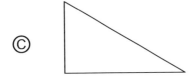

Ⓓ

24   Draw a line on each shape below to show the line of symmetry.

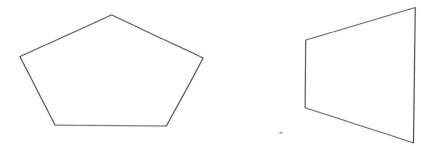

25   Thomas scored 5 times as many points in a basketball game as Jarrod. If Jarrod's number of points is represented as x, which of these shows Thomas's number of points?

Ⓐ $5 + x$

Ⓑ $5 - x$

Ⓒ $\dfrac{5}{x}$

Ⓓ $5x$

END OF SESSION 1

PARCC End-of-Year Assessment

Practice Test 2

Session 2

Instructions

Read each question carefully. For each multiple-choice question, fill in the circle for the correct answer. For other types of questions, follow the directions given in the question.

You may use a ruler and a protractor to help you answer questions. You may not use a calculator on this test.

---

26   Which of the following is a right triangle?

Ⓐ

Ⓑ

Ⓒ

Ⓓ

27   Madison used $1\frac{3}{4}$ cups of milk to make a milkshake. Which of the following is another way to write $1\frac{3}{4}$?

Ⓐ $\frac{1}{4} + \frac{3}{4}$

Ⓑ $\frac{4}{4} + \frac{3}{4}$

Ⓒ $\frac{1 \times 3}{4}$

Ⓓ $\frac{4 \times 3}{4}$

28 Andy was buying a used car. He had four cars in his price range to choose from. The four cars had the odometer readings listed below.

Car	Toyota	Ford	Honda	Saturn
Reading (miles)	22,482	21,987	23,689	22,501

Place the cars in order from the lowest reading to the highest reading. Write the names of the cars below.

Lowest _____

_____

_____

Highest _____

29 Which number goes in the box to make the equation below true? Write your answer in the box below.

$$44 \div \boxed{} = 11$$

30 Which of the following has a mass of about 1 gram?

Ⓐ A dictionary

Ⓑ A pen

Ⓒ A car

Ⓓ A paper clip

31 Shade the model below to show a fraction equivalent to $\frac{6}{10}$.

32 Jade made a pattern using marbles. The first four steps of the pattern are shown below.

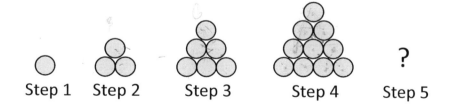

If Jade continues the pattern, how many marbles will she need for Step 5? Write your answer below.

_____

33 A bookstore sold 40,905 books in May. Which of these is another way to write 40,905?

    Ⓐ   Four thousand nine hundred and five

    Ⓑ   Forty thousand ninety five

    Ⓒ   Four thousand ninety five

    Ⓓ   Forty thousand nine hundred and five

34 The thermometers below show the air temperature at 10 a.m. and 2 p.m. one day.

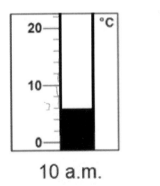 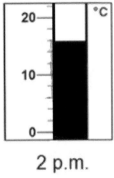

    10 a.m.   2 p.m.

How much did the temperature rise by from 10 a.m. to 2 p.m.?

    Ⓐ   5°C

    Ⓑ   6°C

    Ⓒ   10°C

    Ⓓ   16°C

35 Which **two** pairs of numbers correctly complete this table? Select the **two** correct answers.

Number	Number × 10
850	8,500
3,501	35,010
19	190

☐
28	208

☐
365	36,500

☐
1,987	19,870

☐
6	600

☐
495	4,950

☐
8,700	870

36 The model below shows $2\frac{8}{100}$ shaded.

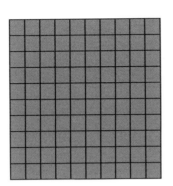 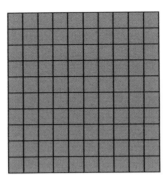 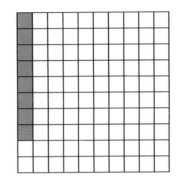

What decimal represents the shaded part of the model? Write your answer below.

_____

37 Joy started a hike at 1:50. It took Joy 2 hours and 25 minutes to finish the hike. What time did Joy finish the hike?

Ⓐ   3:35

Ⓑ   3:50

Ⓒ   4:05

Ⓓ   4:15

38   Ronald competed in a swimming race. All the students finished the race in between 42.5 seconds and 47.6 seconds. Which of the following could have been Ronald's time?

    Ⓐ   41.9 seconds

    Ⓑ   40.5 seconds

    Ⓒ   46.8 seconds

    Ⓓ   48.1 seconds

39   Which procedure can be used to find the next number in the sequence?

$$120, 60, 30, 15, \ldots$$

    Ⓐ   Subtract 15 from the previous number

    Ⓑ   Add 15 to the previous number

    Ⓒ   Multiply the previous number by 2

    Ⓓ   Divide the previous number by 2

40   In each list below, circle the measurement that is the greatest.

    List 1:   1 centimeter   1 kilometer   1 meter

    List 2:   1 ounce   1 gram   1 pound

41   Kevin is 1.45 meters tall. Brad is 20 centimeters taller than Kevin. What is Brad's height? Write your answer below.

_____ centimeters

42   Camilla bought 4 bags of apples. Each bag weighed $\frac{3}{8}$ pounds. What was the total weight of the apples?

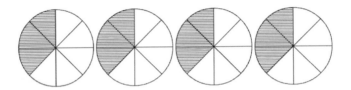

(A)   3 pounds

(B) $1\frac{1}{2}$ pounds

(C) $1\frac{1}{8}$ pounds

(D) $\frac{7}{8}$ pounds

43   Each number in Set P is related in the same way to the number beside it in Set Q.

Set P	Set Q
2	8
6	12
8	14
10	16

When given a number in Set P, what is one way to find its related number in Set Q?

Ⓐ   Multiply by 4

Ⓑ   Multiply by 2

Ⓒ   Add 6

Ⓓ   Add 8

44   In which of these does the number 8 make the equation true?

Ⓐ $48 \div \square = 6$

Ⓑ $\square \div 6 = 48$

Ⓒ $48 \times 6 = \square$

Ⓓ $\square \times 48 = 6$

45 There are 30,854 people living in Montville. Complete the missing numbers to show another way to write 30,854.

$$(10{,}000 \times \boxed{3}) + (100 \times \boxed{}) + (10 \times \boxed{}) + (1 \times \boxed{})$$

46 What does the circled area of the diagram show?

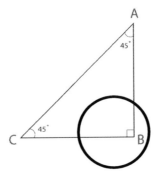

(A) A ray

(B) An angle

(C) A line segment

(D) A point

47 The line plot below shows how many goals each member of a soccer team scored in the season.

Soccer Goals

```
X     X
X     X     X
X     X     X     X
X     X     X     X     X
─────────────────────────────
0     1     2     3     4
```

Which statement is true?

Ⓐ   Each player scored at least 1 goal.

Ⓑ   Only one player scored more than 3 goals.

Ⓒ   The same number of players scored 2 goals as scored 3 goals.

Ⓓ   More players scored 1 goal than scored no goals.

48 The population of Greenville is 609,023. What does the 9 in this number represent?

Ⓐ   Nine thousand

Ⓑ   Ninety thousand

Ⓒ   Nine hundred thousand

Ⓓ   Ninety

49 Place the numbers listed below in order from lowest to highest.

35.061   35.101   35.077   35.009

Lowest   _____

_____

_____

Highest   _____

50 Which fraction and decimal is plotted on the number line below? Circle the **two** correct answers.

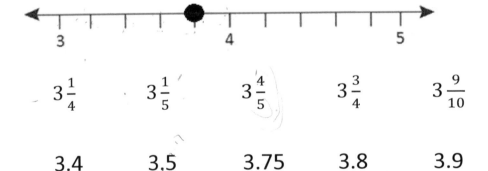

$3\frac{1}{4}$ $3\frac{1}{5}$ $3\frac{4}{5}$ $3\frac{3}{4}$ $3\frac{9}{10}$

3.4   3.5   3.75   3.8   3.9

END OF SESSION 2

ANSWER KEY

Common Core State Standards

The state of Illinois has adopted the Common Core State Standards. Student learning throughout the year is based on these standards, and all the questions on the state tests assess these standards. Just like the real PARCC assessments, the questions in this book test whether students have the knowledge and skills described in the Common Core State Standards.

Assessing Skills and Knowledge

The skills listed in the Common Core State Standards are divided into five topics, or clusters. These are:

- Operations and Algebraic Thinking
- Number and Operations in Base Ten
- Number and Operations – Fractions
- Measurement and Data
- Geometry

The answer key identifies the topic for each question. Use the topics listed to identify general areas of strength and weakness. Then target revision and instruction accordingly.

The answer key also identifies the specific math skill that each question is testing. Use the skills listed to identify skills that the student is lacking. Then target revision and instruction accordingly.

Scoring Constructed Response Questions

This practice test book includes constructed response questions, where students provide a written answer to a question or complete a task. These questions are often scored based on the final answer given as well as the work shown. When asked to show work, students may show calculations, use diagrams, or explain their thinking or process in words. Any form of work that shows the student's understanding can be accepted. Other questions are scored based on tasks completed, explanations given, or justifications given. Answers are provided for these questions, as well as guidance on how to score the questions.

PARCC Performance-Based Assessment, Practice Test 1, Session 1

Question	Answer	Topic	Common Core Skill
1	A, C, T, W	Geometry	Identify line-symmetric figures and draw lines of symmetry.
2	B	Geometry	Draw points, lines, line segments, rays, angles (right, acute, obtuse), and perpendicular and parallel lines. Identify these in two-dimensional figures.
3	B	Measurement & Data	Use the four operations to solve word problems involving money.
4	B	Measurement & Data	Use the four operations to solve word problems involving time.
5	C, P, C, C, P, C	Operations/Algebraic Thinking	Determine whether a given whole number in the range 1–100 is prime or composite.
6	C	Number & Operations-Fractions	Decompose a fraction into a sum of fractions with the same denominator in more than one way, recording each decomposition by an equation. Justify decompositions, e.g., by using a visual fraction model.
7	2,320 2,280	Number & Operations in Base Ten	Compare two multi-digit numbers based on meanings of the digits in each place.
8	See Below	Operations/Algebraic Thinking	Solve multistep word problems posed with whole numbers and having whole-number answers using the four operations.
9	See Below	Measurement & Data	Use the four operations to solve word problems involving time.
10	See Below	Measurement & Data	Within a single system of measurement, express measurements in a larger unit in terms of a smaller unit.
11	See Below	Number & Operations in Base Ten	Compare two multi-digit numbers based on meanings of the digits in each place, using >, =, and < symbols to record the results of comparisons.
12	See Below	Number & Operations in Base Ten	Fluently add and subtract multi-digit whole numbers using the standard algorithm.
13	See Below	Measurement & Data	Solve addition and subtraction problems to find unknown angles on a diagram in real world and mathematical problems.
14	See Below	Measurement & Data	Use the four operations to solve word problems, including problems that require expressing measurements given in a larger unit in terms of a smaller unit. Represent measurement quantities using diagrams such as number line diagrams that feature a measurement scale. Apply the area and perimeter formulas for rectangles in real world and mathematical problems.
15	See Below	Operations/Algebraic Thinking	Find all factor pairs for a whole number in the range 1–100.

Q8.
Answer
6 weeks

Work
The work should show the calculation of 8 × 12 = 96 and 96 ÷ 16 = 6.

Scoring Information
Give a total score out of 3.
Give a score of 1 for the correct answer.
Give a score out of 2 for the working.

Q9.
Answer
3 hours 50 minutes

Work
The student may find the time from 9:30 to midday and then add the time from midday to 1:20, find the hours from 9:30 to 12:30 and then add the minutes from 12:30 to 1:20, find the hours from 9:30 to 1:30 and then subtract 10 minutes, or find the minutes from 9:30 to 1:20 and then convert the time to hours and minutes.

Scoring Information
Give a total score out of 3.
Give a score of 1 for the correct answer.
Give a score out of 2 for the working.

Q10.
Answer
20,000 ml

Work
The work should show an understanding that there are 1,000 milliliters in a liter, and show the calculation of 20 × 1,000 = 20,000.

Scoring Information
Give a total score out of 3.
Give a score of 1 for the correct answer.
Give a score out of 2 for the working.

Q11.
Part A
1,461 < 1,469 < 1,487 < 1,510

Part B
Answer
1,710

Work
The work could show the calculation of 1510 + 200 = 1710. The work could also show increasing the number in the hundreds place by 2.

Scoring Information
Give a total score out of 4.
Give a score of 0.5 for each number correctly ordered in Part A.
Give a score of 1 for the correct answer in Part B.
Give a score out of 1 for the working in Part B.

Q12.
Part A
Answer
5,147

Work
The work should show the calculation of 2,629 + 2,518 = 5,147.

Part B
Answer
111

Work
The work should show the calculation of 2,629 − 2,518 = 111.

Scoring Information
Give a total score out of 4.
Give a score of 1 for the correct answer to Part A.
Give a score out of 1 for the working in Part A.
Give a score of 1 for the correct answer in Part B.
Give a score out of 1 for the working in Part B.

Q13.
Answer
55°

Work
The work should show an understanding that there are 180° in a triangle and subtract 90° and 35° from 180° to give the missing angle measure of 55°.

Scoring Information
Give a total score out of 3.
Give a score of 1 for the correct answer.
Give a score out of 2 for the working.

Q14.
Answer
6 square feet

Work
The work should use each square of the diagram to represent 6 inches or 0.5 feet, and represent the area to be tiled as below.

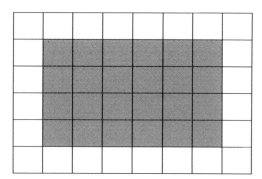

The student may count the squares as 6 square feet or could calculate 2 feet × 3 feet = 6 square feet.

Scoring Information
Give a total score out of 3.
Give a score of 1 for the correct answer.
Give a score out of 2 for the working.

Q15.
Answer
1, 2, 5, 10

Work
The work may list the factors of each number, may show factor trees, or may show an understanding that 10 is a factor of 20 and 40, and so all the factors of 10 are common factors of 10, 20, and 40.

Explanation
The student should explain that 10 is a factor of 20 and 40, so all the factors of 10 are also factors of 20 and 40.

Scoring Information
Give a total score out of 4.
Give a score of 1 for the correct answer. Give a score of 0.5 if only 2 or 3 of the common factors are identified or if additional numbers are incorrectly listed as factors.
Give a score out of 1 for the working.
Give a score out of 2 for the explanation.

PARCC Performance-Based Assessment, Practice Test 1, Session 2

Question	Answer	Topic	Common Core Skill
16	oval, rectangle	Operations/Algebraic Thinking	Generate a number or shape pattern that follows a given rule.
17	D	Number & Operations-Fractions	Compare two fractions with different numerators and different denominators. Justify the conclusions, e.g., by using a visual fraction model.
18	460,000 458,000	Number & Operations in Base Ten	Use place value understanding to round multi-digit whole numbers to any place.
19	A	Measurement & Data	Know relative sizes of measurement units within one system of units.
20	$0.76	Measurement & Data	Use the four operations to solve word problems involving money.
21	C	Number & Operations in Base Ten	Recognize that in a multi-digit whole number, a digit in one place represents ten times what it represents in the place to its right.
22	B	Geometry	Identify line-symmetric figures and draw lines of symmetry.
23	See Below	Number & Operations-Fractions	Understand decimal notation for fractions, and compare decimal fractions.
24	See Below	Number & Operations-Fractions	Build fractions from unit fractions by applying and extending previous understandings of operations on whole numbers.
25	See Below	Operations/Algebraic Thinking	Generate a number or shape pattern that follows a given rule. Identify apparent features of the pattern that were not explicit in the rule itself.
26	See Below	Geometry	Recognize a line of symmetry for a two-dimensional figure as a line across the figure such that the figure can be folded along the line into matching parts.
27	See Below	Number & Operations in Base Ten	Read and write multi-digit whole numbers using base-ten numerals, number names, and expanded form.
28	See Below	Number & Operations in Base Ten	Multiply a whole number of up to four digits by a one-digit whole number using strategies based on place value and the properties of operations.
29	See Below	Measurement & Data	Apply the area and perimeter formulas for rectangles in real world and mathematical problems.
30	See Below	Geometry	Classify two-dimensional figures based on the presence or absence of parallel or perpendicular lines, or the presence or absence of angles of a specified size.

Q23.
Part A
The student should plot a point at 1.75, as shown below.

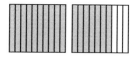

Part B
Answer
$1\frac{3}{4}$ or $1\frac{75}{100}$

Explanation
The student may describe using the number line to determine the fraction, or may describe a numerical conversion of the decimal to a fraction.

Scoring Information
Give a total score out of 4.
Give a score of 1 for the correct answer to Part A.
Give a score of 1 for the correct answer to Part B.
Give a score out of 2 for the explanation.

Q24.
Part A
The model should be shaded as shown below.

Part B
Answer
$\frac{17}{10}$

Explanation
The student may describe using the model to determine the improper fraction, or may describe a numerical conversion.

Scoring Information
Give a total score out of 4.
Give a score of 1 for the correct answer to Part A.
Give a score of 1 for the correct answer to Part B.
Give a score out of 2 for the explanation.

Q25.
Part A
Answer
41

Part B
The student should explain that each number in the pattern is 6 more than the one before it, and that the next number is found by adding 6 to the last number, 35.

Part C
The student should identify that every number in the pattern will be odd. The explanation should show an understanding that every step involves adding an even number to an odd number.

Scoring Information
Give a total score out of 6.
Give a score of 1 for the correct answer in Part A.
Give a score out of 2 for the explanation in Part B.
Give a score of 1 for correctly identifying that every number will be odd in Part C.
Give a score out of 2 for the explanation in Part C.

Q26.
Part A
The isosceles triangle in the center should be identified as the shape that has a line of symmetry. A line of symmetry should be drawn on the triangle, as shown below.

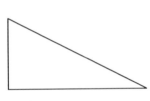 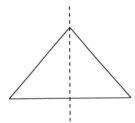 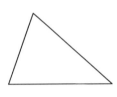

Part B
Explanation
The student may describe how the two halves are the same size and shape or how the two halves can be folded onto each other.

Scoring Information
Give a total score out of 4.
Give a score of 1 for the correct shape identified.
Give a score of 1 for the line of symmetry drawn correctly.
Give a score out of 2 for the explanation.

Q27.
Part A

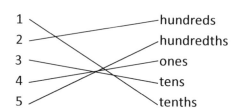

Part B

$2 \times 100 + 3 \times 10 + 4 \times 1 + 1 \times \frac{1}{10} + 5 \times \frac{1}{100}$

Scoring Information
Give a total score out of 4.
Give a score out of 2 for Part A.
Give a score out of 2 for Part B.

Q28.
Answer
156

Work
The work should show the calculation of 26 × 6 = 156.

Scoring Information
Give a total score out of 3.
Give a score of 1 for the correct answer.
Give a score out of 2 for the working.

Q29.
Answer
2,400 square feet

Work
The work should show the calculation of 60 × 40 = 2,400.

Scoring Information
Give a total score out of 3.
Give a score of 1 for the correct answer.
Give a score out of 2 for the working.

Q30.
The column for 1 or more right angles should list A, C, and D.
The column for 1 or more pairs of parallel sides should list A, D, E, and F.
The column for 1 or more pairs of perpendicular sides should list A, C, and D.

Scoring Information
Give a total score out of 3.
Give a score of 1 for each column correctly completed.

PARCC End-Of-Year Assessment, Practice Test 1, Session 1

Question	Answer	Topic	Common Core Skill
1	26 cm 30 cm^2	Measurement & Data	Apply the area and perimeter formulas for rectangles in real world and mathematical problems.
2	4, 9	Operations/Algebraic Thinking	Recognize that a whole number is a multiple of each of its factors.
3	Fruit juice, Quiche	Measurement & Data	Use the four operations to solve word problems involving money.
4	B	Operations/Algebraic Thinking	Solve multistep word problems posed with whole numbers and having whole-number answers using the four operations.
5	B	Operations/Algebraic Thinking	Assess the reasonableness of answers using mental computation and estimation strategies including rounding.
6	960 beads	Number & Operations in Base Ten	Multiply a whole number of up to four digits by a one-digit whole number using strategies based on place value and the properties of operations.
7	A	Number & Operations-Fractions	Apply and extend previous understandings of multiplication to multiply a fraction by a whole number.
8	165°	Measurement & Data	Measure angles in whole-number degrees using a protractor.
9	A	Number & Operations in Base Ten	Find whole-number quotients and remainders with up to four-digit dividends and one-digit divisors.
10	D	Operations/Algebraic Thinking	Find all factor pairs for a whole number in the range 1–100.
11	12, 14, 30, 54, 66	Operations/Algebraic Thinking	Determine whether a given whole number in the range 1–100 is a multiple of a given one-digit number.
12	255,000 grams	Measurement & Data	Within a single system of measurement, express measurements in a larger unit in terms of a smaller unit.
13	C	Number & Operations-Fractions	Use decimal notation for fractions with denominators 10 or 100.
14	6	Measurement & Data	Record measurement equivalents in a two-column table.
15	C	Geometry	Draw and identify right, acute, and obtuse angles.
16	D	Measurement & Data	Know relative sizes of measurement units within one system of units.
17	A	Number & Operations in Base Ten	Read and write multi-digit whole numbers using base-ten numerals, number names, and expanded form.
18	A	Operations/Algebraic Thinking	Generate and analyze patterns.
19	3rd and 6th	Measurement & Data	Use the four operations to solve word problems involving money.
20	6	Number & Operations in Base Ten	Find whole-number quotients using strategies based on place value, the properties of operations, and/or the relationship between multiplication and division.

21	D	Measurement & Data	Within a single system of measurement, express measurements in a larger unit in terms of a smaller unit.
22	D	Operations/Algebraic Thinking	Assess the reasonableness of answers using mental computation and estimation strategies including rounding.
23	C	Number & Operations in Base Ten	Recognize that in a multi-digit whole number, a digit in one place represents ten times what it represents in the place to its right.
24	1st, 3rd, and 4th	Geometry	Identify line-symmetric figures and draw lines of symmetry.
25	D	Number & Operations-Fractions	Compare two decimals to hundredths by reasoning about their size.

PARCC End-Of-Year Assessment, Practice Test 1, Session 2

Question	Answer	Topic	Common Core Skill
26	57, 247, 121, 93	Operations/Algebraic Thinking	Determine whether a given whole number in the range 1–100 is prime or composite.
27	4th and 5th	Number & Operations-Fractions	Compare two fractions with different numerators and different denominators.
28	C	Operations/Algebraic Thinking	Generate and analyze patterns.
29	64 square inches	Measurement & Data	Apply the area and perimeter formulas for rectangles in real world and mathematical problems.
30	Q and T R and S	Geometry	Identify perpendicular and parallel lines in two-dimensional figures.
31	B	Measurement & Data	Know relative sizes of measurement units within one system of units.
32	D	Number & Operations in Base Ten	Read and write multi-digit whole numbers using base-ten numerals, number names, and expanded form.
33	2.4	Number & Operations-Fractions	Use decimal notation for fractions with denominators 10 or 100.
34	A	Number & Operations in Base Ten	Read and write multi-digit whole numbers using base-ten numerals, number names, and expanded form.
35	C	Measurement & Data	Solve addition and subtraction problems to find unknown angles on a diagram.
36	77, 81, 91	Operations/Algebraic Thinking	Determine whether a given whole number in the range 1–100 is prime or composite.
37	83,500 83,460	Number & Operations in Base Ten	Use place value understanding to round multi-digit whole numbers to any place.
38	60 and 6,000 6 and 600	Number & Operations in Base Ten	Recognize that in a multi-digit whole number, a digit in one place represents ten times what it represents in the place to its right.
39	D	Measurement & Data	Measure angles in whole-number degrees using a protractor.
40	$1.36	Measurement & Data	Use the four operations to solve word problems involving money.
41	D	Geometry	Identify perpendicular and parallel lines in two-dimensional figures.
42	C	Number & Operations-Fractions	Recognize and generate equivalent fractions.
43	B	Number & Operations-Fractions	Compare two decimals to hundredths by reasoning about their size.
44	B	Number & Operations-Fractions	Solve word problems involving multiplication of a fraction by a whole number.
45	D	Operations/Algebraic Thinking	Assess the reasonableness of answers using mental computation and estimation strategies including rounding.
46	24	Operations/Algebraic Thinking	Solve multistep word problems posed with whole numbers and having whole-number answers using the four operations.
47	D	Number & Operations in Base Ten	Fluently add and subtract multi-digit whole numbers using the standard algorithm.
48	72	Number & Operations in Base Ten	Multiply a whole number of up to four digits by a one-digit whole number.
49	A	Operations/Algebraic Thinking	Solve multistep word problems posed with whole numbers and having whole-number answers using the four operations.
50	A	Operations/Algebraic Thinking	Represent problems using equations with a letter standing for the unknown quantity.

PARCC Performance-Based Assessment, Practice Test 2, Session 1

Question	Answer	Topic	Common Core Skill
1	D	Measurement & Data	Know relative sizes of measurement units within one system of units.
2	X, M, L	Geometry	Draw points, lines, line segments, rays, angles (right, acute, obtuse), and perpendicular and parallel lines. Identify these in two-dimensional figures.
3	C	Number & Operations-Fractions	Use decimal notation for fractions with denominators 10 or 100.
4	C	Number & Operations in Base Ten	Find whole-number quotients using strategies based on place value, the properties of operations, and/or the relationship between multiplication and division.
5	Any 4 segments shaded	Number & Operations-Fractions	Explain why a fraction is equivalent to a fraction by using visual fraction models.
6	B	Operations/Algebraic Thinking	Generate and analyze patterns.
7	589 < 596 805 > 799 152 < 170	Number & Operations in Base Ten	Compare two multi-digit numbers based on meanings of the digits in each place, using >, =, and < symbols to record the results of comparisons.
8	See Below	Number & Operations-Fractions	Express a fraction with denominator 10 as an equivalent fraction with denominator 100, and use this technique to add two fractions with respective denominators 10 and 100.
9	See Below	Operations/Algebraic Thinking	Solve multistep word problems posed with whole numbers and having whole-number answers using the four operations, including problems in which remainders must be interpreted.
10	See Below	Number & Operations in Base Ten	Fluently add and subtract multi-digit whole numbers using the standard algorithm.
11	See Below	Number & Operations-Fractions	Decompose a fraction into a sum of fractions with the same denominator in more than one way, recording each decomposition by an equation. Justify decompositions, e.g., by using a visual fraction model.
12	See Below	Measurement & Data	Apply the area and perimeter formulas for rectangles in real world and mathematical problems.
13	See Below	Measurement & Data	Use the four operations to solve word problems involving money.
14	See Below	Geometry	Draw points, lines, line segments, rays, angles (right, acute, obtuse), and perpendicular and parallel lines. Identify these in two-dimensional figures.
15	See Below	Operations/Algebraic Thinking	Solve multistep word problems posed with whole numbers and having whole-number answers using the four operations, including problems in which remainders must be interpreted. Represent these problems using equations with a letter standing for the unknown quantity.

Q8.
Answer

$$\frac{13}{100}$$

Work

The work should show converting $\frac{1}{10}$ to $\frac{10}{100}$, and then calculating $\frac{10}{100} + \frac{3}{100} = \frac{13}{100}$.

Scoring Information

Give a total score out of 3.
Give a score of 1 for the correct answer.
Give a score out of 2 for the working.

Q9.
Answer

10 pencils

Work

The work should show the calculation of $82 \div 8 = 10$ remainder 2.

Scoring Information

Give a total score out of 3.
Give a score of 1 for the correct answer.
Give a score out of 2 for the working.

Q10.
Answer

718

Work

The work should show the calculation of $254 + 235 + 229 = 718$.

Scoring Information

Give a total score out of 3.
Give a score of 1 for the correct answer.
Give a score out of 2 for the working.

Q11.
Part A

The last grid of the model should have 3 of the 4 parts shaded.

Part B
Answer

$$\frac{3}{4}$$

Explanation

The explanation should refer to the diagram showing that 3 of the 4 parts of the whole are shaded.

Scoring Information

Give a total score out of 4.
Give a score of 1 for the correct shading in Part A.
Give a score of 1 for the correct answer in Part B.
Give a score out of 2 for the explanation.

Q12.
Answer
4 square inches or 4 in^2

Work
The work should show the side length as 2 inches, and show the calculation of 2 inches × 2 inches = 4 square inches.

Scoring Information
Give a total score out of 4.
Give a score of 1 for the correct numerical answer of 4.
Give a score of 1 for the correct units of square inches or in^2.
Give a score out of 2 for the working.

Q13.
Answer
15 nickels

Work
The work may show that each quarter is equal to 25 cents, or 5 nickels, and then show 5 × 3 = 15. The work may also show that the quarters are equal to 75 cents, and a nickel is equal to 5 cents, and then show the calculation 75 ÷ 5 = 15.

Scoring Information
Give a total score out of 3.
Give a score of 1 for the correct answer.
Give a score out of 2 for the working.

Q14.
Part A
The two smallest angles should be circled.

Part B
The student should refer to how you can tell that the angles are less than a right angle.

Scoring Information
Give a total score out of 4.
Give a score of 1 for each correct angle circled.
Give a score out of 2 for the explanation.

Q15.
Part A
$c = 2d + 4$

Part B
Answer
$16

Work
The work should show substituting $d = 6$ into the equation $c = 2d + 4$ and solving it as below.
$c = 2(6) + 4 \rightarrow c = 12 + 4 \rightarrow c = 16$

Scoring Information
Give a total score out of 6.
Give a score out of 2 for the equation in Part A.
Give a score of 1 for the correct answer in Part B.
Give a score of 1 for using the correct value of $d = 6$ in Part B.
Give a score out of 2 for the working in Part B.

PARCC Performance-Based Assessment, Practice Test 2, Session 2

Question	Answer	Topic	Common Core Skill
16	3	Operations/Algebraic Thinking	Generate and analyze patterns.
17	C	Measurement & Data	Know relative sizes of measurement units within one system of units.
18	32 and 56	Operations/Algebraic Thinking	Determine whether a given whole number in the range 1–100 is a multiple of a given one-digit number.
19	B	Number & Operations-Fractions	Understand addition and subtraction of fractions as joining and separating parts referring to the same whole.
20	35 hours	Operations/Algebraic Thinking	Multiply or divide to solve word problems involving multiplicative comparison.
21	B	Measurement & Data	Understand concepts of angle measurement, including that an angle is measured with reference to a circle with its center at the common endpoint of the rays, and that an angle that turns through 1/360 of a circle is called a "one-degree angle," and can be used to measure angles.
22	C	Measurement & Data	Within a single system of measurement, express measurements in a larger unit in terms of a smaller unit.
23	See Below	Operations/Algebraic Thinking	Multiply or divide to solve word problems involving multiplicative comparison.
24	See Below	Measurement & Data	Sketch angles of specified measure.
25	See Below	Operations/Algebraic Thinking	Determine whether a given whole number in the range 1–100 is prime or composite.
26	See Below	Measurement & Data	Apply the area and perimeter formulas for rectangles in real world and mathematical problems.
27	See Below	Number & Operations-Fractions	Express a fraction with denominator 10 as an equivalent fraction with denominator 100, and use this technique to add two fractions with respective denominators 10 and 100.
28	See Below	Number & Operations-Fractions	Use decimal notation for fractions with denominators 10 or 100.
29	See Below	Measurement & Data	Use the four operations to solve word problems involving intervals of time, including problems involving simple fractions or decimals, and problems that require expressing measurements given in a larger unit in terms of a smaller unit.
30	See Below	Geometry	Classify two-dimensional figures based on the presence or absence of parallel or perpendicular lines, or the presence or absence of angles of a specified size.

Q23.
Part A
Answer
6

Work
The work should show that 6 is the greatest number that divides evenly into 12, 18, and 24.

Part B
Answer
4

Work
The work may show the calculation of 24 ÷ 6 = 4, or could use a diagram to represent 6 piles of 4 pennies each.

Scoring Information
Give a total score out of 6.
Give a score of 1 for the correct answer to Part A.
Give a score out of 2 for the working in Part A.
Give a score of 1 for the correct answer to Part B.
Give a score out of 2 for the working in Part B.

Q24.
The student should sketch a labeled right angle with an angle equal to 90°.
The student should sketch a labeled acute angle with an angle less than 90°.
The student should sketch a labeled obtuse angle with an angle greater than 90°.

Explanation
The explanation should show an understanding that the right angle must be 90°, while the other two angles do not have to be an exact measure.

Scoring Information
Give a total score out of 6.
Give a score of 1 for each angle correctly sketched.
Give a score of 1 for identifying that the right angle had to be exact.
Give a score out of 2 for the explanation.

Q25.
Answer
23, 29

Explanation
The student should explain that prime numbers can only be divided by themselves and 1, while composite numbers can be divided by at least one other number.

Scoring Information
Give a total score out of 4.
Give a score of 1 for each number correctly listed. Take off 1 point for each additional number incorrectly listed.
Give a score out of 2 for the explanation.

Q26.
Part A
Answer
240 feet

Work
The work should show the calculation of 80 + 80 + 40 + 40 = 240 or (2 × 80) + (2 × 40) = 240.

Part B
Answer
80 yards

Work
The work should show an understanding that there are 3 feet in 1 yard.
The work should show the calculation of 240 ÷ 3 = 80.

Scoring Information
Give a total score out of 6.
Give a score of 1 for the correct answer to Part A.
Give a score out of 2 for the working in Part A.
Give a score of 1 for the correct answer to Part B.
Give a score out of 2 for the working in Part B.

Q27.
Answer
$\frac{47}{100}$

Work
The student should shade 30 of the 100 squares to represent $\frac{3}{10}$ and 17 of the 100 squares to represent $\frac{17}{100}$.

Scoring Information
Give a total score out of 3.
Give a score of 1 for the correct answer.
Give a score out of 2 for the working.

Q28.
Answer
0.7

Work
The work could show dividing 70 by 100 or could show simplifying $\frac{70}{100}$ to $\frac{7}{10}$ and then writing $\frac{7}{10}$ as 0.7.

Scoring Information
Give a total score out of 3.
Give a score of 1 for the correct answer.
Give a score out of 2 for the working.

Q29.
Answer
105 minutes

Work
The work could show calculating $1\frac{3}{4} \times 60$ or could show calculating $60 + (\frac{3}{4} \times 60)$.

Scoring Information
Give a total score out of 3.
Give a score of 1 for the correct answer.
Give a score out of 2 for the working.

Q30.
Part A
The statements "2 pairs of parallel sides" and "4 congruent sides" should be circled.

Part B
square

Scoring Information
Give a total score out of 3.
Give a score of 1 for each correct statement circled in Part A. Take off 1 point if additional statements are circled.
Give a score of 1 for the correct answer in Part B.

PARCC End-of-Year Assessment, Practice Test 2, Session 1

Question	Answer	Topic	Common Core Skill
1	165 minutes	Measurement & Data	Use the four operations to solve word problems involving time.
2	B	Operations/Algebraic Thinking	Solve multistep word problems posed with whole numbers and having whole-number answers using the four operations, including problems in which remainders must be interpreted.
3	D	Operations/Algebraic Thinking	Find all factor pairs for a whole number in the range 1–100. / Determine whether a given whole number in the range 1–100 is prime or composite.
4	$6 \times t = 42$	Operations/Algebraic Thinking	Represent problems using equations with a letter standing for the unknown quantity.
5	C	Number & Operations-Fractions	Understand addition and subtraction of fractions as joining and separating parts referring to the same whole.
6	5	Operations/Algebraic Thinking	Find all factor pairs for a whole number in the range 1–100.
7	B	Operations/Algebraic Thinking	Assess the reasonableness of answers using mental computation and estimation strategies including rounding.
8	A	Operations/Algebraic Thinking	Solve multistep word problems posed with whole numbers and having whole-number answers using the four operations.
9	C	Measurement & Data	Use the four operations to solve word problems involving money.
10	C	Measurement & Data	Know relative sizes of measurement units within one system of units.
11	2nd, 5th, 6th	Operations/Algebraic Thinking	Find all factor pairs for a whole number in the range 1–100. / Determine whether a given whole number in the range 1–100 is prime or composite.
12	÷ 3	Operations/Algebraic Thinking	Generate and analyze patterns.
13	D	Number & Operations in Base Ten	Recognize that in a multi-digit whole number, a digit in one place represents ten times what it represents in the place to its right.
14	7 people	Measurement & Data	Solve problems by using information presented in line plots.
15	Any 2 segments shaded	Number & Operations-Fractions	Understand, recognize, and generate equivalent fractions using visual fraction models, with attention to how the number and size of the parts differ even though the two fractions themselves are the same size.
16	0.14	Number & Operations-Fractions	Use decimal notation for fractions with denominators 10 or 100.
17	A	Number & Operations-Fractions	Record the results of comparisons with symbols >, =, or <, and justify the conclusions, e.g., by using a visual fraction model.
18	C	Operations/Algebraic Thinking	Assess the reasonableness of answers using mental computation and estimation strategies including rounding.

19	24 pints 48 cups	Measurement & Data	Within a single system of measurement, express measurements in a larger unit in terms of a smaller unit.
20	B	Measurement & Data	Solve addition and subtraction problems to find unknown angles on a diagram in real world and mathematical problems.
21	A	Operations/Algebraic Thinking	Generate and analyze patterns.
22	A	Number & Operations-Fractions	Use decimal notation for fractions with denominators 10 or 100.
23	C	Geometry	Identify perpendicular and parallel lines in two-dimensional figures.
24	Vertical line at center of pentagon, horizontal line at center of trapezoid	Geometry	Identify line-symmetric figures and draw lines of symmetry.
25	D	Operations/Algebraic Thinking	Represent verbal statements of multiplicative comparisons as multiplication equations.

PARCC End-of-Year Assessment, Practice Test 2, Session 2

Question	Answer	Topic	Common Core Skill
26	A	Geometry	Recognize right triangles as a category, and identify right triangles.
27	B	Number & Operations-Fractions	Decompose a fraction into a sum of fractions with the same denominator in more than one way, recording each decomposition by an equation.
28	Ford Toyota Saturn Honda	Number & Operations in Base Ten	Compare two multi-digit numbers based on meanings of the digits in each place.
29	4	Number & Operations in Base Ten	Find whole-number quotients using strategies based on place value, the properties of operations, and/or the relationship between multiplication and division.
30	D	Measurement & Data	Know relative sizes of measurement units within one system of units.
31	Any 3 segments shaded	Number & Operations-Fractions	Understand, recognize, and generate equivalent fractions using visual fraction models, with attention to how the number and size of the parts differ even though the two fractions themselves are the same size.
32	15	Operations/Algebraic Thinking	Generate and analyze patterns.
33	D	Number & Operations in Base Ten	Read and write multi-digit whole numbers using base-ten numerals, number names, and expanded form.
34	C	Measurement & Data	Represent measurement quantities using diagrams such as number line diagrams that feature a measurement scale.
35	3rd and 5th	Number & Operations in Base Ten	Recognize that in a multi-digit whole number, a digit in one place represents ten times what it represents in the place to its right.
36	2.08	Number & Operations-Fractions	Use decimal notation for fractions with denominators 10 or 100.
37	D	Measurement & Data	Use the four operations to solve word problems involving time.
38	C	Number & Operations-Fractions	Compare two decimals to hundredths by reasoning about their size.
39	D	Operations/Algebraic Thinking	Generate and analyze patterns.
40	1 kilometer 1 pound	Measurement & Data	Know relative sizes of measurement units within one system of units.
41	165 centimeters	Measurement & Data	Use the four operations to solve word problems involving distances, including problems involving simple fractions or decimals.
42	B	Number & Operations-Fractions	Solve word problems involving multiplication of a fraction by a whole number.
43	C	Operations/Algebraic Thinking	Generate and analyze patterns.
44	A	Number & Operations in Base Ten	Find whole-number quotients using strategies based on place value, the properties of operations, and/or the relationship between multiplication and division.

45	3, 8, 5, 4	Number & Operations in Base Ten	Read and write multi-digit whole numbers using base-ten numerals, number names, and expanded form.
46	B	Measurement & Data	Recognize angles as geometric shapes that are formed wherever two rays share a common endpoint.
47	B	Measurement & Data	Solve problems by using information presented in line plots.
48	A	Number & Operations in Base Ten	Recognize that in a multi-digit whole number, a digit in one place represents ten times what it represents in the place to its right.
49	35.009 35.061 35.077 35.101	Number & Operations-Fractions	Compare two decimals to hundredths by reasoning about their size.
50	$3\frac{4}{5}$, 3.8	Number & Operations-Fractions	Use decimal notation for fractions with denominators 10 or 100.

38586172R00077

Made in the USA
Charleston, SC
13 February 2015